CW00551053

Copycat Recipes

How to create the Most Famous Restaurants' Recipes, Eating Healthily, Tasty and without High Costs

Sarah Miller

Table of contents

Introduction

Cooking at home can be time-consuming and create a mess you need to clean up, but once you prepare a particular dish and eat it, you will be proud and amazed to have made a popular snack - a delicious meal with your own hands.

Preparing your favorite dishes at home is now easy. In this volume, you will find proven recipes from your favorite fast-food restaurant Cracker Barrel, Subway, Taco Bell, and Burger King. With these recipes, you will have the same final flavor by saving money and having fun. All the recipes here are easy to follow, and the ingredients are not hard to find! It is much cheaper to buy your ingredients for your dishes at the local farmer market.

This is the best book for making imitation homemade recipes. The recipes give an accurate measurement of the ingredients, but you can modify some of them depending on how you prefer the flavor. Whether you want to minimize spice or add more to your food is up to you. You can get rid of the ingredients you are allergic to or use ingredients with lower sugar or fat content. The possibilities are endless. You have full control over that.

Chapter 1

Breakfast and Brunch

Waffle House's Waffle

Preparation Time: 5 minutes

Cooking Time: 20 minutes

Servings: 6

Ingredients

- 11/2cups of all-purpose flour
- 1 teaspoon of salt
- 1/2teaspoon of baking soda
- 1 egg
- 1/2cup + 1 tablespoon of granulated white sugar
- 2 tablespoons of butter, softened
- 2 tablespoons of shortening
- 1/2cup of half-and-half
- 1/2cup of milk
- 1/4cup of buttermilk
- 1/4teaspoon of vanilla

Directions

1. Prepare the dry mixture by sifting the flour into a bowl and mixing it with soda's salt and bicarbonate.
2. In a medium bowl, lightly beat an egg when the egg has become frothy, hammer in the butter, sugar, and shortening.
3. When the mixture is thoroughly mixed, hammer in the half-and-half, vanilla, milk, and buttermilk, continue beating the mixture until it's smooth.
4. While beating the wet mixture, slowly pour in the dry mix to combine thoroughly and take away all the lumps.
5. Chill the batter overnight (optional but recommended; if you can't chill the mixture overnight, leave it for 15 to twenty minutes).
6. Take the batter out of the refrigerator. Preheat and grease your waffle iron.
7. Cook each waffle for 3 to four minutes. Serve with butter and syrup.

Nutrition:

Calories 313.8,

Total Fat 12.4g,

Carbohydrates 45g,

Protein 5.9g

Sodium 567.9mg

Mimi's Café Santa Fé Omelet

Preparation Time: 10 minutes

Cooking Time: 10 minutes

Servings: 1

Ingredients

Chipotle Sauce:

- 1 cup of marinara or tomato sauce
- 3/4 cup of water
- 1/2cup of chipotle in adobo sauce
- 1 teaspoon of kosher salt Omelet:
- 1 tablespoon of onions, diced
- 1 tablespoon of jalapeños, diced
- 2 tablespoons of cilantro, chopped
- 2 tablespoons of tomatoes, diced
- 1/4cup of fried corn tortillas, cut into strips
- 3 eggs, beaten
- 2 slices cheese 1 dash of salt and pepper Garnish:
- 2 ounces of chipotle sauce, hot
- 1/4cup of fried corn tortillas, cut into strips
- 1 tablespoon of sliced green onions
- 1 tablespoon of guacamole

Directions

1. Melt some butter in a pan over medium heat, ensuring to coat the whole pan.
2. Sauté the jalapeños, cilantro, tomatoes, onions, and tortilla strips for a few minutes.
3. Add the eggs, seasoning them with salt and pepper and stirring occasionally.
4. Flip the omelet when it's set. Place the cheese in the highest half.
5. When the cheese starts to become melty, fold the omelet in half and transfer to a plate.
6. Garnish the omelet with chipotle sauce, guacamole, green onions, and corn tortillas.

Nutrition:

Calories 519,

Total Fat 32g,

Carbohydrates 60g,

Protein 14g,

Sodium 463 mg

Alice Springs Chicken from Outback

Preparation Time: 5 minutes

Cooking Time: 2 hours 30 minutes

Servings: 4

Ingredients

Sauce:

- 1/2cup Dijon mustard
- 1/2cup honey
- 1/4cup mayonnaise
- 1 teaspoon fresh lemon juice

Chicken Preparation:

- 4 chicken breast, boneless and skinless
- 2 tablespoons of butter
- 1 tablespoon olive oil
- 8 ounces fresh mushrooms, sliced
- 4 slices bacon, cooked and cut into 2-inch pieces
- 2 1/2cups of Monterrey Jack cheese, shredded
- Parsley for serving (optional)

Directions

1. Preheat oven to 400 °F.
2. Mix ingredients for the sauce in a bowl.
3. Put the chicken in a Ziploc bag, and then add the sauce into the bag until only 1/4cup is left. Keep the remaining sauce in a container, cover, and refrigerate. Confirm to seal Ziploc bag tightly and gently shake until chicken is coated with sauce confine refrigerator for a minimum of 2 hours.
4. Melt butter in a pan over medium heat. Add mushrooms and cook for five minutes or until brown. Remove from pan and place on a plate.
5. Heat oil in an oven-safe pan. Place marinated chicken flat in the pan and cook for five minutes on all sides or until each side turns golden brown.
6. Top with even amounts of mushroom, bacon, and cheese. Cover pan with an oven-safe lid then bakes for 10 to fifteen minutes until chicken is cooked through. Remove lid and bake a further 1-3 minutes until the cheese is all melted.
7. Transfer onto a plate. Serve with remaining sauce on the side. Sprinkle chicken with parsley if desired

Nutrition:

Calories 888

Total Fat 56g

Carbohydrates 41g

Protein 59g

Sodium 1043mg

Oriental Salad from Applebee's

Preparation Time: 15 minutes

Cooking Time: 5 minutes

Servings: 6

Ingredients

- 3 tablespoons of honey
- 11/2tablespoons of rice wine vinegar
- 1/4cup of mayonnaise
- 1 teaspoon Dijon mustard
- 1/8 teaspoon sesame oil
- 3 cups of vegetable oil, for frying
- 2 chicken breasts, cut into thin strips
- 1 egg
- 1 cup of milk
- 1 cup of flour
- 1 cup breadcrumbs
- 1 teaspoon salt
- 1/4teaspoon pepper
- 3 cups of romaine lettuce, diced
- 1/2cup of red cabbage, diced
- 1/2cup of napa cabbage, diced
- 1 carrot, grated
- 1/4cup of cucumber, diced

- 3 tablespoons of sliced almonds
- 1/4cup of dry chow mein
-

Directions

1. To make the dressing, add honey, rice vinegar, mayonnaise, Dijon mustard, and vegetable oil to a blender. Mix until well combined. Store in refrigerator until able to serve.
2. Heat oil in a deep pan over medium-high heat.
3. As the oil warms, whisk together egg and milk in a bowl. In another bowl, add flour, breadcrumbs, salt, and pepper. Mix well.
4. Dredge chicken strips in egg mixture, then in the flour mixture. Confirm the chicken is coated evenly on all sides. Shake off any excess.
5. Deep fry chicken strips for about 3 to 4 minutes until thoroughly cooked and lightly brown. Transfer onto a plate lined with paper towels to empty and funky. Add batches, if necessary. Chop strips into small, bite-sized pieces once cool enough to handle.
6. Next, prepare the salad by adding romaine, red cabbage, napa cabbage, carrots, and cucumber to a serving bowl. Top with chicken pieces, almonds, and dish. Drizzle prepared to dress on top.
7. Serve immediately.

Nutrition:

Calories 384Total

Fat 13g Saturated

Fat 3g

Carbohydrates 40g

Sugar 13g

Fibers 2g

Protein 27g

Sodium 568 Mg

Panda Express Bacon Muffins

Preparation time: 5 min

Cooking time: 15 minutes

Servings: 4

Ingredients:

- 12.7oz flour
- Salt Pepper
- *Egg*
- 1 tsp parsley
- Four bacon pieces
- 7.8fl oz. milk
- *Onion*
- 2 tbsp. olive oil
- 3.5ounce Cheddar cheese
- 2 tablespoon of powder

Directions:

1. Preheat oven to 190C/170C fan-forced. Line a 12-hole, 1/3 cup–capacity muffin pan with paper cases.
2. Heat oil in a medium frying pan over medium-high heat. Add bacon. Cook for five minutes or until crisp. Cool.

3. Combine sifted flour with pepper, cheese, chives, and bacon in a medium bowl. Make a well in the center. Add remaining ingredients, stirring until combined.
4. Spoon mixture into paper cases. Bake for 20-25 minutes or until golden and just firm to the touch. Substitute pan for five minutes. Transfer to a wire rack to chill.

Nutrition:

Calories: 350

Fat: 18g

Carbohydrates: 32g

Protein: 16g

Chapter 2

Appetizers and Drinks

Red Lobster Takeout Dry Garlic Ribs

Preparation Time: 10 minutes

Cooking time: 30 minutes

Servings: 6

Ingredients:

- 6 pounds pork ribs, silver skin removed and cut into individual ribs
- 11/2cups broth
- 11/2cups brown sugar
- 1/4cup soy sauce
- 12 cloves garlic, minced
- 1/4cup yellow mustard
- 1 large onion, finely chopped
- 1/4teaspoon salt
- 1/2teaspoon black pepper

Directions:

1. Preheat oven to 200°F.
2. Season ribs with salt and pepper and place on a baking tray. Cover with aluminum foil and bake for 1 hour.
3. In a mixing bowl, stir together the broth, brown sugar, soy sauce, garlic, mustard and onion. Continue stirring until the sugar is completely dissolved.
4. After an hour, remove the foil from the ribs and turn the heat up to 350°F.
5. Carefully pour the sauce over the ribs. Re-cover with the foil and return to the oven for 1 hour.
6. Remove the foil and bake for 15 more minutes on each side.

Nutrition:

Calories 228,

Total Fat 15 g,

Carbs 12 g,

Protein 13 g,

Sodium 418 mg

Panda Express Mini Crab Cakes

Preparation time: 10 minutes

Cooking time 4 minutes

Servings: 4

Ingredients:

- 2 tablespoons mayonnaise
- 2 tablespoons green onion, minced (green part only)
- 2 tablespoons red bell pepper, minced
- 1/2beaten egg
- 1 teaspoon fresh parsley, minced
- 1 teaspoon Old Bay seasoning
- 1/2teaspoon prepared yellow mustard
- 1/2pound lump crab meat

- 3 tablespoons plain breadcrumbs
- 1/4cup panko breadcrumbs
- vegetable oil

Remoulade Sauce:

- 1/2cup mayonnaise
- 2 teaspoons capers
- 2 teaspoons dill pickle slices, chopped
- 1 teaspoon lemon juice
- 1/2teaspoon fresh parsley, minced
- 1/2teaspoon paprika
- 1/2teaspoon chili powder
- 1/4teaspoon cayenne pepper
- 1/4teaspoon ground cumin
- 1/8 teaspoon salt

Directions:

1. In a large bowl, combine the mayo, green onions, red pepper, egg, parsley, Old Bay, mustard, crab meat, and the plain bread crumbs.
2. Gently mix the ingredients together. Don't over mix or the crab meat will fall apart too much.
3. Working carefully, form the mixture into 4 equal-sized flat patties.

4. Cover the patties with parchment paper and refrigerate for a couple of hours. Refrigerating will help the patty to set.
5. In the meantime, mix all of the Remoulade sauce ingredients together, making sure it is well combined.
6. After the crab cakes have had a chance to chill, heat enough oil in a large skillet so that the crab cake has enough to sit in.
7. Pour the panko breadcrumbs in a shallow dish and dip each crab cake into the panko, then place it in the skillet and cook for 2 to 3 minutes on each side. Remove the crab cakes from the skillet and allow them to drain on a paper towel. Serve with the remoulade sauce.

Nutrition:

Calories: 289

Fat: 8.7 g

Carbs: 25. 2 g

Protein: 33.9 g

Sodium: 331 mg

Panda Express Avocado Egg Rolls

Preparation time: 15 minutes

Cooking time 5 minutes

Servings: 8

Ingredients:

- 3 avocados, halved, peeled and seeded
- 1 Roma tomato, diced
- 1/4cup diced red onion
- 2 tablespoons chopped fresh cilantro leaves

- Juice of 1 lime
- Kosher salt and freshly ground black pepper, to taste
- 1 cup vegetable oil
- 8 egg roll wrappers

Cilantro Dipping Sauce:

- 3/4 cup fresh cilantro leaves, loosely packed
- 1/3 cup sour cream
- 1 jalapeño, seeded and deveined (optional)
- 2 tablespoons mayonnaise
- 1 clove garlic
- Juice of 1 lime
- Kosher salt and freshly ground black pepper, to taste

Directions:

1. First, mix all of the ingredients for the cilantro dipping sauce, and set it aside.
2. In a medium mixing bowl, mash the avocados up a bit with the back of a fork. Gently mix in the tomato, onion, cilantro, lime juice, salt, and pepper.
3. In a deep skillet or saucepan, heat the vegetable oil over medium to high heat.
4. Take your egg roll wrappers and fill each one with some of the avocado mixture. Fold the sides over, and then fold down the top and bottom. You can wet your fingers and dampen the wrapper to seal the seams.

5. When the oil is heated, add the egg rolls and fry until they turn a beautiful golden brown. Then remove them and place them on a paper towel to drain.
6. Serve with cilantro dipping sauce.

Nutrition:

Calories: 266

Fat: 9.8 g

Carbs: 32. 1 g

Protein: 24.2 g

Sodium: 309 mg

Red Lobster Sweet Corn Cakes

Preparation time: 15 minutes

Cooking time 15 minutes

Servings: 4

Ingredients:

For the Salsa Verde:

- 2 tomatillos, roughly chopped
- 1 (4 -ounce) can diced green chilies, drained
- 1 green onion, sliced thin
- 2 tablespoons fresh cilantro, roughly chopped
- 1 1/2teaspoons granulated sugar
- 1/4teaspoon ground cumin
- 1/4teaspoon salt
- 1/8 teaspoon ground black pepper

For the Pico De Gallo:

- 1 large Roma tomato, diced
- 1 tablespoon red onion, diced
- 1 tablespoon fresh cilantro, minced
- 1/2teaspoon lime juice
- Salt and ground pepper to taste

For Southwestern Sauce:

- 1/2cup mayonnaise
- 1 teaspoon white vinegar
- 1 teaspoon water
- 1/2teaspoon granulated sugar
- 1/2teaspoon chili powder
- 1/4teaspoon paprika
- 1/8 teaspoon cayenne pepper
- 1/4teaspoon onion powder
- 1/8 teaspoon garlic powder

For the Corn Cakes:

- 1 1/2cups frozen sweet corn, divided
- 1/2cup butter, softened to room temperature
- 3 tablespoons sugar
- 1/8 teaspoon salt
- 1/2cup corn masa harina flour
- 2 tablespoons all-purpose flour
- 1 1/2tablespoons olive oil

For Garnish:

- Sour cream
- Avocado, diced
- Fresh cilantro, chopped

Directions:

1. First, make the Salsa Verde. Pulse the ingredients for the Salsa Verde in the blender so it is roughly combined.
2. Make the Pico de Gallo and Southwestern Sauce by combining the ingredients together. When they are all well combined, cover them and put them in the refrigerator.
3. Prepare the corn cakes. First, place 1 cup of corn in the blender or food processor and purée.
4. Combine the puréed corn, butter, sugar, salt in a medium bowl, and mix it.
5. In a small bowl, combine the masa and flour and stir.
6. Add the remaining corn and masa mixture to the butter and corn mixture and then form into patties.
7. Heat the oil in a large skillet over medium-low to medium heat. When oil is hot, add the corn cakes and fry on each side for about 5 to 8 minutes.

8. Serve with the salsa Verde, Pico de Gallo and Southwestern sauce for dipping. Garnish with sour cream, avocado, and cilantro.

Nutrition:

Calories: 320

Fat: 16.6 g

Carbs: 30. 1 g

Protein: 21.6 g

Sodium: 452 mg

Red Lobster Fried Mac and Cheese Balls

Preparation time:15 minutes

Cooking time 15 minutes

Servings: 6

Ingredients:

Sauce:

- 1 3/4 cups marinara sauce
- 1 3/4 cups alfredo sauce
- 1/4cup heavy whipping cream
- 1 teaspoon garlic powder
- 1/2cup ricotta cheese
- 1 cup Italian blend shredded cheese

- 1/4cup red wine

Balls:

- 16 ounces grated white sharp cheddar, grated
- 16 ounces smoked gouda cheese, grated
- 3 tablespoons butter
- 2 tablespoons flour
- 2 cups whole milk, warmed
- 1-pound large elbow macaroni, cooked
- Salt and pepper, to taste
- 3 eggs
- 3 tablespoons milk
- 3 cups panko bread crumbs
- Fresh Parmesan cheese for garnish only
- vegetable oil for frying

Directions:

1. Make the balls. In a mixing bowl, combine the shredded cheddar and shredded gouda.
2. In a large saucepan, melt the butter. Add the flour slowly, whisking until there are no lumps. Gradually add the 2 cups of warm milk. Whisk until smooth, and continue cooking until the sauce begins to thicken.
3. When the sauce is thickened, remove it from the heat and gradually mix in the cheddar and gouda cheeses.

Stir until the cheese is melted and incorporated thoroughly.

4. Add the cooked macaroni and salt and pepper into the cheese sauce and stir well.
5. Butter a large cake pan, spread the mac and cheese mixture evenly into the pan, and then place it in the refrigerator for at least two hours. You want the mixture to set and make it easier to form into balls.
6. After two hours, remove the tray from the refrigerator and form the mac and cheese into evenly sized balls about 2 inches in diameter. Cover, and put them in the freezer for at least an hour.
7. In a small bowl, beat your eggs and 3 tablespoons of milk together.
8. Place the bread crumbs in a shallow dish.
9. In a deep skillet or large saucepan, heat enough vegetable oil so that the balls will be covered when you fry them.
10. When the oil is heated to 350°F, dip each ball in the egg mixture, then the panko crumbs, and drop them into oil. Work in batches, and cook until the balls are a nice golden brown color, about 3–4 minutes. Transfer to paper towel as they finish cooking to drain.
11. Make your cheese sauce by combining the marinara and alfredo sauce in a small saucepan. Heat over medium

and when warm, add the ricotta, Italian cheese blend, and wine. Stir to combine.

12. When the cheeses have melted, remove the pot from the heat and add the garlic powder and heavy cream. Stir well.
13. Serve the macaroni balls with the cheese sauce and a sprinkle of Parmesan.

Nutrition:

Calories: 200

Fat: 14.4 g

Carbs: 37. 5 g

Protein: 28.8 g

Sodium: 430 mg

Chapter 3

Pasta and Soup Recipes

Panera Creamy Tomato Soup

Preparation Time: 10 minutes

Cooking Time: 15 minutes

Servings: 3

Ingredients:

- 2 tbsp. olive oil
- 1 cup white onions, chopped
- 2 tsp. garlic, minced
- 60 ounces' tomato puree
- 2 tsp. basil, dried
- 1/2 tsp. oregano
- 15 ounces' vegetable stock
- 1/2 cup cream
- 1 tsp. sugar
- Salt to taste

- Black pepper to taste

Directions:

1. In a saucepan, add olive oil and heat over medium heat and chopped white onion. Sprinkle of salt on top. Sauté until transparent to the onions.
2. Add the chopped garlic and sauté until fragrant.
3. Tomatoes puree, basil, vegetable stock, oregano, and heavy cream are added. Reduce to simmer oil. Simmer for 9-10 minutes.
4. Nice taste, and apply sugar if the soup is too acid.
5. You can make puree soup with either an electric mixer or in a blender.
6. Season it with salt and black pepper.

Nutrition:

Calories: 361

Fat: 44.9 g

Carbs: 85. 6 g

Protein: 16.8 g

Sodium: 494 mg

Olive Garden Pasta e Fagioli

Preparation Time: 10 minutes

Cooking time: 25 minutes

Servings: 8

Ingredients:

- 1 cup ditalini pasta
- Two tablespoons olive oil, divided
- Three cloves garlic, minced
- One onion, diced
- Three carrots, peeled and diced
- 1-pound spicy Italian sausage, casing removed
- Two stalks celery, diced
- 3 cups chicken broth
- One teaspoon dried oregano
- 3/4 teaspoon dried thyme
- 1 (16-ounce) can tomato sauce
- 1 (15-ounce) can diced tomatoes
- One teaspoon dried basil
- Black pepper and Kosher salt as per taste
- One can(15-ounce) red kidney beans, drained and rinsed

- One can(15-ounce) Great Northern beans, drained and rinsed

Directions:

1. Cook pasta according to package instructions in a large pot of boiling salted water; drain well, and set aside.
2. Now you heat one tablespoon of olive oil over medium heat in a big stockpot or Dutch oven. Pour Italian sausage to the skillet and cook for around 3-5 minutes until browned, making sure the sausage crumbles as it cooks; remove excess fat and set aside.
3. Add one tablespoon of oil remaining to stockpot. Add garlic, onions, carrots and celery. Cook for about 3-4 minutes, stirring periodically, until tender.
4. Whisk in a broth of chicken, tomato sauce, diced tomatoes, basil, oregano, thyme, Italian sausage and 1 cup of water; season to taste with salt and pepper. Make to a boil; reduce heat and cook, covered, for about 10-15 minutes, until vegetables are tender.
5. Stir in the beans and pasta until heated.
6. Serve immediately.

Nutrition:

Calories: 267

Fat: 5.9 g

Carbs: 6. 6 g

Protein: 43.8 g

Sodium: 178 mg

Red Lobster's Shrimp Pasta

Preparation Time: 5 minutes

Cooking Time: 30 minutes

Servings: 4

Ingredients

- 8 ounces of linguini or spaghetti pasta
- 1/3 cup of extra virgin olive oil
- 3 garlic cloves
- 1-pound of shrimp, peeled, deveined
- 2/3 cup of clam juice or chicken broth
- 1/3 cup of white wine
- 1 cup of heavy cream
- 1/2cup of Parmesan cheese, freshly grated
- 1/4teaspoon of dried basil, crushed

- 1/4teaspoon of dried oregano, crushed
- Fresh parsley and Parmesan cheese for garnish

Directions

1. Cook the Pasta consistent with package directions.
2. Simmer the garlic in hot oil over low heat until tender.
3. Increase the warmth from low to medium and add the shrimp. When the shrimp is cooked, transfer it to a separate bowl alongside the garlic. Keep the remaining oil in the pan.
4. Pour the clam or chicken stock into the pan and convey it to a boil.
5. Add the wine and adjust the warmth to medium. Keep cooking the mixture for an additional 3 minutes.
6. While stirring the mixture, reduce the warmth to low and add in the cream and cheese. Keep stirring.
7. When the mixture thickens, return the shrimp to the pan and contribute the remaining ingredients (except the pasta).
8. Place the pasta in a bowl and pour the sauce over it.
9. Mix and serve. Garnish with parsley and parmesan cheese, if desired

Nutrition:

Calories: 590,

Total Fat: 26 g,

Carbs: 54 g,

Protein: 34 g,

Sodium: 1500 mg

Cheesecake Factory's Cajun Jambalaya Pasta

Preparation Time: 10 minutes

Cooking Time: 40 minutes

Servings: 4

Ingredients

Cajun Seasoning Blend:

- 1 teaspoon of white pepper
- 1 teaspoon of cayenne pepper
- 3 teaspoons of salt
- 1 teaspoon of paprika
- 1/2teaspoon of garlic powder
- 1/2teaspoon of onion powder

Chicken and Shrimp:

- 2 boneless skinless chicken breasts, halved, cut into bite-size pieces
- 1/2pound of large shrimp, peeled, deveined
- 1 tablespoon of olive oil

Pasta:

- 5 quarts water
- 6 ounces of fettuccine
- 6 ounces of spinach fettuccine

Jambalaya:

- 1 tablespoon of olive oil
- 2 medium tomatoes, chopped
- 1 medium onion, sliced
- 1 green bell pepper, sliced
- 1 red bell pepper, sliced
- 1 yellow bell pepper, sliced
- 11/2cups of chicken stock
- 1 tablespoon of cornstarch
- 2 tablespoons of white wine
- 2 teaspoons of arrowroot powder
- 2 teaspoons of fresh parsley, chopped

Directions

1. Mix all of the Cajun seasoning blend ingredients to form the seasoning. Divide the spices into three equal parts.
2. Coat the chicken and shrimp with 1/3 of the seasoning each.
3. Cook pasta consistent with package directions.
4. While expecting the pasta, sauté the spiced chicken in heated oil in a large skillet.
5. When the chicken starts turning brown, stir in the shrimp and cook until the chicken is cooked through and the shrimp turn pink.

6. Transfer the chicken and shrimp to a plate and put aside.
7. Using an equivalent pan, warm the oil for the jambalaya over medium heat. Add the tomatoes, onions, peppers, and remaining 1/3 of the seasoning mix. Sauté for 10 minutes.
8. When the vegetables turn brownish-black, add the chicken and shrimp back to the combination.
9. Pour in 3/4 cup of the chicken broth to deglaze the pan. Gently scrape the pan to get rid of the burnt particles. Turn the warmth to high and permit the mixture to cook.
10. When the broth has evaporated completely, add in the remaining stock and cook for an additional 5 minutes.
11. Turn the warmth right down to low and leave the mixture to rest and overheat. In a bowl, mix the wine and arrowroot until it dissolves.
12. Add the mixture to the jambalaya. Turn the warmth to low and leave the mixture to simmer.
13. When the jambalaya and pasta are done, assemble the dish by:
14. Putting the pasta because the first layer;
15. Covering the pasta with the jambalaya sauce, and garnish each plate with parsley.

Nutrition:

Calories: 563.9,

Total Fat: 13.3 g,

Carbs: 73.8 g,

Protein: 35.9 g,

Sodium: 1457.6 mg

California Pizza Kitchen's Kung Pao Spaghetti

Preparation Time: 10 minutes

Cooking time 10 minutes

Servings 4–6

Ingredients

- 1 cup of chicken stock
- 4 tablespoons of cornstarch, divided
- 3/4 cup of soy sauce
- 1/2cup of sherry
- 3 tablespoons of chili paste with garlic
- 1/4cup of sugar
- 2 tablespoons of red wine vinegar
- 2 tablespoons of sesame oil
- 2 egg whites
- 1/2teaspoon of salt
- 1-pound of spaghetti
- 1/4cup of olive oil
- 1-pound of boneless skinless chicken breast, cut into 3/4-inch cubes
- 10–15 whole Chinese dried red chili peppers; DO NOT eat them for color and heat!
- 1 cup of unsalted dry roasted peanuts

- 1/4cup garlic, minced
- 3 cups green onions, greens, and white parts, coarsely chopped

Directions

1. Make the sauce by whisking together the chicken broth and a couple of tablespoons of cornstarch. Stir until the cornstarch dissolves.
2. Whisk in the soy, sherry, chili paste, sugar, vinegar, and vegetable oil. Bring back a boil.
3. Turn the warmth down and simmer until the sauce thickens about 20 minutes.
4. In a small bowl, whisk together the egg whites, two tablespoons of cornstarch, and salt. Stir until well blended, but not such a lot that the egg whites froth.
5. Bring salted water to a quick boil in a large pot. Add the pasta and cook until almost hard. Drain.
6. Heat the vegetable oil in a large skillet over medium-high heat.
7. Add the cut chicken pieces to the albumen mixture and stir to coat. Carefully add the chicken and albumen mixture to the skillet to make a "pancake." Cook until the egg sets, then flip and cook on the opposite side. Separate the chicken pieces.
8. When the chicken pieces turn golden brown, stir in the garlic and scallions and cook for about 30 seconds. Add

the sauce that you simply made earlier and go to ensure it covers everything. Add the pasta and stir to mix with the sauce.

Nutrition:

Calories: 890,

Total Fat: 37g,

Carbs: 112g,

Protein: 28g,

Fiber: 9g

Chapter 4

Sides and Salads

Cracker Barrel's Brussels Sprouts N' Kale Salad

Preparation Time: 5 minutes Cooking Time: 0 minutes Servings: 6

Ingredients:

- 1 bunch kale
- 1 pound Brussels sprouts
- 1/4cup craisins (or dry cranberries)
- 1/2cup pecans, chopped

Maple vinaigrette:

- 1/2cup olive oil
- 1/4cup apple cider vinegar
- 1/4cup maple syrup
- 1 teaspoon dry mustard

Directions:

1. Slice the kale and Brussels sprouts with a cheese grater or mandolin slicer. Transfer to a salad bowl.
2. Add the pecans to a skillet on high heat. Toast for 60 seconds, then transfer to the salad bowl.
3. Add the craisins.
4. Mix all of the ingredients for the vinaigrette and whisk to combine.
5. Pour the vinaigrette over the salad and toss. Refrigerate for a few hours or preferably overnight before serving.

Nutrition:

Calories 211,

Total Fat 6 g,

Carbs 4 g,

Protein 7 g,

Panda Express Cinnamon Apples

Preparation Time: 10 minutes

Cooking time: 10 minutes

Servings: 3

Ingredients:

- 1/4cup butter
- 1/2cup apple cider
- 1 tablespoon cornstarch
- 2 pounds Golden Delicious apples, cored, peeled and cut into wedges
- 1 teaspoon lemon juice
- 1 teaspoon cinnamon
- 1/8 teaspoon nutmeg
- 1/8 teaspoon allspice
- 1/4cup brown sugar

Directions:

1. In a large skillet, melt your butter over a medium to medium-low heat. Add the apples in a single layer, then top with the lemon juice followed by the brown sugar and spices.
2. Cover, reduce the heat to low, and allow the apples to simmer until tender.

3. Transfer the apples from the skillet to a serving bowl, leaving the juices in the skillet.
4. Whisk 1/2cup of the juice together with the cornstarch in a small bowl. Turn the heat under the skillet up to medium-high and whisk the cornstarch mixture into the rest of the juices. Stir constantly until it thickens and there are no lumps.
5. Pour the juice over the bowl of apples and stir to coat.

Nutrition:

Calories 115

Protein 35

Carbs 26

Fat 5

Cracker Barrel's Coleslaw

Preparation Time: 10 minutes

Cooking time: 0 minutes

Servings: 3

Ingredients:

- 2 cups shredded cabbage
- 1/2cup shredded carrots
- 1/2cup shredded purple cabbage
- 1 cup Miracle Whip
- 1 teaspoon celery seeds
- 1/2teaspoon salt
- 1/2teaspoon pepper
- 1/3 cup sugar
- 1/4cup vinegar
- 1/4cup buttermilk
- 1/4cup milk
- 4 teaspoons lemon juice

Directions:

1. Toss the carrots and cabbages in a large mixing bowl.

2. Stir in the Miracle Whip, celery seeds, salt, pepper, sugar, vinegar, buttermilk, milk, and lemon juice. Toss again to combine completely.
3. Refrigerate for about 3 hours before serving.

Nutrition:

Calories 215

Protein 35

Carbs 26

Fat 5

Panda Express Lima Beans

Preparation Time: 10 minutes

Cooking time: 30 minutes

Servings: 2

Ingredients:

- 1 cup water
- 1 chicken bouillon cube
- 2 slices bacon, chopped
- 1 clove garlic, peeled and lightly mashed
- 1/2teaspoon red pepper flakes
- 1/2teaspoon onion powder
- 1 teaspoon sugar
- 1/2teaspoon black pepper
- 1 (1-pound) bag frozen lima beans

Directions:

1. Add the water and bouillon cube to a large pot and bring to a boil.
2. Stir in the remaining ingredients. Cover and turn the heat down so that the beans are simmering slightly.
3. Allow to simmer for 30 minutes, stirring occasionally. (Add more water if necessary.)
4. Remove the garlic and then, season with salt and pepper to taste.

Nutrition:

Calories 115

Protein 35

Carbs 26

Fat 5

Olive Garden Green Beans

Preparation Time: 10 minutes

Cooking time: 35 minutes

Servings: 3

Ingredients:

- 4 slices thick-cut bacon, chopped into pieces
- 1 (14½-ounce) can cut green beans in water (do not drain)

- 1/2cup onion, finely diced
- 1 teaspoon sugar
- Salt
- Pepper

Directions

1. Add the bacon to a large saucepan and cook over medium heat until it is browned but not yet crispy.
2. Stir in the green beans (with liquid), onion and sugar. Bring to a boil, then reduce heat and simmer for 30–35 minutes.
3. Season to taste and serve.

Nutrition:

Calories 215

Protein 37

Carbs 26

Fat 5

Chapter 5

Bread and Pizzas

Cracker Barrel Bacon Cheeseburger

Servings: 6-8

Preparation Time: 15 minutes

Cooking Time: 30-35 minutes

Ingredients

- 1 pizza crust of choice
- 1/2-3/4 cup basic or marinara sauce
- 4 strips bacon
- 1/2 pound hamburger
- 1/2 small onion chopped
- Salt and pepper, to taste
- 1 1/2 cup mozzarella
- 1/2 cup cheddar, shredded
- 1/2 tomato sliced or chopped

Directions

1. Preheat oven 425 degrees F.

2. Heat bacon strips in skillet or non-stick frying pan over medium heat until browned and almost crisp. Cool and chop into bite size pieces. Set aside.
3. Drain off any bacon drippings in excess of 2 Tablespoons. If needed, add a bit of olive oil. Add the hamburger meat and bacon. Season with salt and pepper. Stir-fry until browned. Remove from heat and let cool.
4. Spread sauce over crust and spread with cheddar cheese.
5. Spread hamburger mixture on top.
6. Sprinkle with shredded mozzarella and top with chopped bacon.
7. Bake until golden brown and bubbly (12-15 minutes).

Nutrition:

Calories 376

Carbs 42 g

Fat 14 g

Protein 23 g

Sodium 1332 mg

Philly Cheesesteak Pizza

Servings: 6-8

Preparation Time: 15 minutes

Cooking Time: 20-22 minutes

Ingredients

- 1 pizza crust of choice
- 1/2-3/4 cup basic or marinara sauce
- 2 ounces cream cheese
- 2 cups provolone cheese, shredded and divided
- 1 cup precooked roast beef, cut into thin strips
- 1/3 cup pickled pepper rings
- 1/4 cup grated Parmesan cheese
- 1/2 teaspoon dried oregano

For pepper mixture:

- 1 Tablespoon olive oil
- 2 small bell peppers (green, red or combination), sliced into thin strips
- 1 1/2 cups sliced fresh mushrooms
- 1 small onion, chopped

Directions

1. Preheat oven to 450 degrees F.

2. Par bake crust until set (about 5 minutes). Remove from oven and let cool.
3. Prepare pepper mixture. Heat oil in a skillet over medium heat and add peppers, mushrooms and onion. Sauté until tender. Remove from heat and let cool.
4. Spread sauce over crust.
5. Scoop cream cheese evenly on top and sprinkle with 1 cup provolone.
6. Add beef, pepper mixture and pepper rings.
7. Sprinkle with remaining provolone, parmesan and oregano.
8. Bake until crust is golden and cheese is melted (about 10-12 minutes).

Nutrition:

Calories 439

Carbs 36 g

Fat 20 g

Protein 29 g

Sodium 826 mg

El Chico's Creamy Bacon

Servings: 6-8

Preparation Time: 15 minutes

Cooking Time: 15-25 minutes

Ingredients

- 1 pizza crust of choice
- 1/2-3/4 cup creamy white sauce with garlic
- 1 cup ricotta
- 6-8 strips bacon, fried crisp, drained on paper towels and chopped
- 1 Tablespoon bacon drippings
- 1/2 cup mushrooms, sliced thinly
- Freshly-ground black pepper, to taste
- Dried thyme (optional)

Directions

1. Preheat oven to 475 degrees F.
2. Bake crust until lightly golden (about 10-15 minutes). Remove from oven and let cool.
3. Heat bacon drippings in a skillet over medium heat and sauté mushrooms until tender and lightly browned (about 3-4 minutes). Remove from heat and drain on paper towels. Let cool slightly.

4. Spread sauce and ricotta over crust.
5. Top with mushroom and bacon.
6. Season with black pepper and sprinkle with thyme (if using).
7. Bake to heat through and brown crust (about 2-5 minutes).
8. Serve immediately.

Nutrition:

Calories 393

Carbs 34 g

Fat 22 g

Protein 15 g

Sodium 434 mg

El Chico's Neopolitan Apollonia Pizza

Servings: 6-8

Preparation Time: 15 minutes

Cooking Time: 3-5 minutes

Ingredients

- 1 thin crust or any dough of choice
- 1 cup mozzarella di bufala
- 2 cloves garlic, sliced very thinly
- 1 cup Italian salami or cured meat like coppa, pancetta or mortadella, chopped
- 2 eggs, beaten
- Coarse sea salt and freshly-ground black pepper, to taste
- Fresh basil leaves
- 1 Tablespoon extra-virgin olive oil
- 1/4 cup parmigiano reggiano, grated
-

Directions

1. Preheat oven to hottest temperature (500-550 degrees F for most home ovens), with rack positioned closest to grill. When well-heated, turn on grill.

2. Place the crust in a heated skillet or non-stick pan and cook until dough begins to puff up and bottom begins to brown (about 60-90 seconds).
3. Transfer to pan or pizza peel.
4. Tear mozzarella di bufala and scatter over dough.
5. Sprinkle with garlic and chopped salami.
6. Drizzle with beaten eggs and season with salt and pepper.
7. Top with basil leaves and drizzle with olive oil.
8. Place under grill and bake until eggs are just set and crust is browned (about 2-5 minutes).
9. Sprinkle with parmigiano reggiano.
10. Serve hot.

Nutrition:

Calories 254

Carbs 23 g

Fat 8 g

Protein 11 g

Sodium 658 mg

Cracker Barrel Sausage & Mushroom

Servings: 6-8

Preparation Time: 15 minutes

Cooking Time: 12 minutes

Ingredients

- 1 thin pizza crust dough
- 1/2 cup basic or marinara pizza sauce
- 8 ounces bulk Italian sausage, cooked and drained
- 1 cup fresh mushrooms, sliced thinly
- 1/8 teaspoon red pepper flakes, or to taste (optional)
- 8 ounces I shredded Italian cheese blend
- Parmesan cheese, grated

Directions

1. Preheat oven to 450 degrees F.
2. Par-bake crust until lightly browned (about 7 minutes). Let cool slightly.
3. Spread sauce over dough.
4. Add sausage and mushrooms.
5. Sprinkle with red pepper flakes (optional).
6. Top with shredded Italian cheese blend.
7. Bake until cheese is melted (about 5 minutes).

8. Remove from heat and sprinkle with grated parmesan.

Nutrition:

Calories 348

Carbs 42 g

Fat 13 g

Protein 18 g

Sodium 1290 mg

Chicago-Style Deep-Dish Pizza

Servings: 8

Prep Time: 20 minutes

Cook Time: 40-50 minutes

Ingredients

- 1 deep dish pizza crust, par-baked to set
- 1-2 Tablespoons butter (optional)
- 2 cups shredded mozzarella (Stella, Frigo or Sorrento), preferably whole-milk, divided
- 1-2 cups filling of choice
- Options for filling (combination of 2 or more, as desired):
- Italian sausage, cooked and crumbled
- pancetta, cooked and crumbled
- pepperoni, sliced thinly
- green pepper, sliced thinly
- yellow onion, sliced
- mushrooms, sliced
- black olives, sliced
- 1 cup basic pizza sauce
- 1/4 cup grated parmesan cheese
- 1-2 Tablespoons olive oil

Directions

1. Preheat oven to 375 degrees F.
2. Par-bake crust just to set (about 5-10 minutes).
3. Brush hot crust with butter, if using.
4. Spread 1/2 cup mozzarella over crust.
5. Mix 1 cup mozzarella with filling and add to crust.
6. Top with remaining mozzarella.
7. Cover with sauce.
8. Sprinkle with parmesan and drizzle with olive oil.
9. Bake until crust is golden brown and top is bubbly (40-50 minutes). Cover loosely with foil if crust browns too quickly.
10. Let set for 15 minutes before slicing.

Nutrition:

Calories 515

Carbs 45 g

Fat 31 g

Protein 18 g

Sodium 1396 mg

Chapter 6

Poultry and Fish Recipes

Taco Bell's Bonefish Grill's Bang-Bang Shrimp

Preparation Time: 5 minutes
Cooking Time: 5 minutes
Servings: 4

Ingredients

- 1/2cup of mayonnaise
- 1/4cup of Thai sweet chili sauce
- 3-5 drops of hot chili sauce (or more if you like it spicier)
- 1/2cup of cornstarch
- 1-pound of small shrimp, peeled and deveined
- 11/2cups of vegetable oil

Directions

1. To make the sauce, combine mayonnaise with Thai condiment and hot condiment in a bowl.
2. In a separate bowl, add cornstarch. Toss shrimp in cornstarch until well-coated.
3. Heat oil in a wok. Work in batches, fry shrimp until golden brown, about 2-3 minutes. Transfer onto a plate lined with paper towels to empty excess oil.
4. Serve shrimp in a bowl with sauce drizzled on top.

Nutrition:

Calories 274,

Total Fat 11 g,

Carbs 26 g,

Protein 16 g,

Sodium 1086 mg

Green Chili Jack Chicken

Preparation Time: 10 minutes

Cooking time: 20 minutes

Servings: 4

Ingredients:

- 1 pound chicken strips
- 1 teaspoon chili powder
- 4 ounces green chilies
- 2 cups Monterey Jack cheese, shredded
- 1/4cup salsa

Direction:

1. Sprinkle the chicken with the chili powder while heating some oil over medium heat.
2. Cook the chicken strips until they are half cooked, and then place the green chilies on top of the chicken. Lower the heat to low.
3. Cook for 1 to 2 minutes before adding the cheese on top. Keep cooking the chicken and cheese until the cheese melts.
4. Serve the chicken with the salsa.

Nutrition:

Calories: 132

Total Fat: 23g

Carbs: 12g

Protein: 81g

Fiber: 0g

Cracker Barrel Honey Grilled Salmon

Preparation Time: 10 minutes

Cooking time 30 minutes

Servings 4

Ingredients

- 1/4cup of honey
- 1/3 cup of soy sauce
- 1/4cup of dark brown sugar, packed
- 1/4cup of pineapple juice
- 2 tablespoons fresh lemon juice
- 1 tablespoon apple cider vinegar
- 1 tablespoon olive oil
- 1 teaspoon ground black pepper, plus more for seasoning the salmon
- 1/2teaspoon cayenne pepper
- 1/2teaspoon paprika
- 1/2teaspoon garlic powder
- 4 (8 ounces) salmon fillets
- Rice and vegetables, to serve

Directions

1. In a medium saucepan over medium-low heat, combine all the ingredients except the fish. Bring it to a boil, then

reduce the warmth, occasionally stirring until the sauce thickens to the consistency of syrup.

2. Cook the salmon to your preference, either on the grill or in the oven.
3. Serve the salmon with sauce over the highest, with rice and vegetables.

Nutrition:

Calories: 233

Total Fat: 14g

Carbs: 36g

Protein: 44g

Fiber: 0g

Ratatouille Tilapia

Preparation Time: 10 minutes

Cooking time 20 minutes

Servings 4

Ingredients

- 2 tablespoons of olive oil
- 1 small eggplant (2 cups), diced
- 1 small zucchini, diced
- 1 sweet green pepper, seeded, cored, and diced
- 1 small onion, diced
- 2 cloves garlic, minced
- 1/2teaspoon salt
- 1/4teaspoon hot pepper flakes
- 1 (19 ounces) can diced tomatoes (or fresh tomatoes if you have them)
- 2 tablespoons of tomato paste
- 1 tablespoon fresh oregano, minced
- 1/3 cup of fresh parsley, minced
- 4 tilapia fillets
- 1/4cup of all-purpose flour
- 2 tablespoons of extra-virgin olive oil

Directions

1. In a large skillet, heat the vegetable oil over medium heat and cook the eggplant, zucchini, sweet pepper, onion, and garlic.
2. Add the salt and hot pepper flakes and cook until the vegetables are soft. Then stir in the tomatoes, ingredient, and oregano. Cook until the mixture thickens a touch, stirring occasionally. Mix in the parsley.
3. While your vegetables are cooking, place the flour in a shallow dish. Dip the tilapia in the flour on each side, and then shake off any excess.
4. Heat 2 tablespoons of additional virgin vegetable oil in a large skillet over medium heat. When the oil is hot, transfer the tilapia to the skillet and cook for 2–3 minutes on all sides. It'll get crispy and golden brown.
5. Place the tilapia fillets on serving dishes and top with the cooked vegetable mixture.

Nutrition:

Calories: 104.4

Total Fat: 5g

Carbs: 2.4g

Protein: 15.1g

Fiber: 4.8g

Taco Bell's Apple Cheddar Chicken

Preparation Time: 10 minutes

Cooking time: 45 minutes

Servings: 4

Ingredients:

- 5 cooked skinless chicken breasts, whole or cubed (Cracker Barrel uses the whole breast, but either option works just as well.)
- 2 cans apple pie filling, cut apples in third
- 1 bag extra-sharp cheddar cheese
- 1 row Ritz crackers, crushed
- 1 cup melted butter

Directions:

1. Preheat the oven to 350°F.
2. Combine the chicken, apple pie filling, and cheddar cheese in a mixing bowl. Stir to combine.
3. Pour the mixture into a greased casserole dish.
4. Mix Ritz crackers with the melted butter. Spread over the casserole.
5. Bake for 45 minutes or until it starts to bubble.

Nutrition:

Calories: 111

Total Fat: 23g

Carbs: 12g

Protein: 81g

Fiber: 0g

Cracker Barrel Shrimp Broccoli Cavatappi

Preparation Time: 10 minutes

Cooking time 15 minutes

Servings 4-6

Ingredients

- 1-pound shrimp, peeled and deveined
- 2 cups dried cavatappi pasta
- 2 cups of broccoli florets
- 1 tablespoon butter
- 2 cloves garlic, minced
- 2 tablespoons of flour
- 1 1/3 cups of milk
- 1 1/4cups of Parmesan cheese, freshly grated, divided
- 2 tablespoons of cream cheese
- 1/4teaspoon salt
- Freshly ground black pepper to taste

Directions

1. Cook the shrimp, either on a hot grill (which will add that wonderful smoky flavor) or just fry them in a skillet. Either way, cook them for about 2–3 minutes on

all sides, just until they turn pink. Keep warm after they need finishing cooking.

2. Cook the pasta in a pot of boiling water until its tender. Everyone likes pasta in a particular way, so cook to your preference.
3. Steam the broccoli.
4. In a large saucepan, melt the butter over medium heat. Add the garlic and cook until fragrant, about 1 minute.
5. Stir in the flour and gradually whisk in the milk. Continue cooking for about 5 minutes, or until it thickens. Add 1 cup of the Parmesan cheese and, therefore, the cheese, and season with salt and pepper. Whisk together until the cheese is melted, and consequently, the mixture is smooth.
6. Add in the cooked pasta and broccoli and stir to make sure everything is coated.
7. Serve plated pasta and broccoli with shrimp on the highest. Add extra Parmesan if you desire.

Nutrition:

Calories: 520

Total Fat: 22g

Carbs: 33g

Protein: 49g

Fiber: 7g

Chapter 7

Beef and Pork Recipes

Café Rio's Sweet Pork Salad

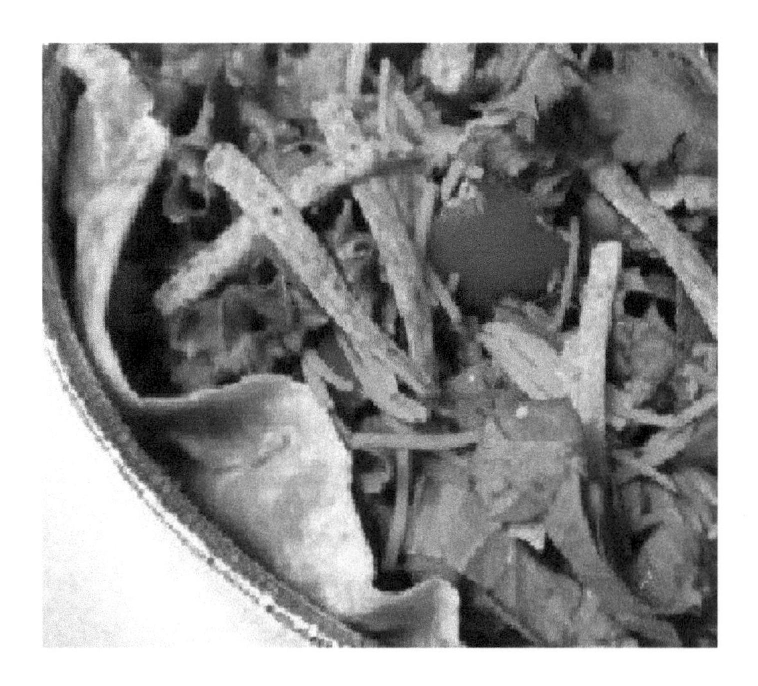

Preparation time: 20 minutes

Cooking time: 5 hours

Servings: 12

Ingredients

- For the Meat
- 6 pounds pork shoulder (yields about 4 pounds cooked, fat removed, shredded pork)
- 1 1/2teaspoons onion salt
- 1/2teaspoon ground black pepper
- 2 cloves garlic, crushed and minced
- 1 can cola (not diet)

For the Sauce

- 2 (4-ounce) cans diced mild to medium green chilies
- 1 1/2cups red enchilada sauce
- 1 cup brown sugar
- 2 cloves garlic, chopped
- 1 can cola

For the Filling

- *Guacamole*
- Café Rio Black Beans
- Cilantro Lime Rice

For serving (optional)

- 6 corn tortillas, sliced into strips and fried
- 12–16 *flour tortillas*, softened (or 1 per serving), warmed
- Lettuce, chopped
- Tomatoes, sliced

- Sweet onion, sliced
- Cheddar or Mexican blend cheese, shredded
- Pico de Gallo OR SALSA
- Sour cream
- Cilantro, chopped

Directions

1. Preheat the oven to 350°F and place the rack in the bottom third (or use a slow cooker).
2. Season the roast with onion salt and black pepper. Rub the garlic on the top of the meat.
3. Place the roast in the roasting pan (or slow cooker) and pour the cola at the bottom.
4. Cover tightly and roast for 2 hours without opening the oven. Reduce the heat to 200°F and bake 3 more hours. (If using a slow cooker, cook on LOW for 5 hours.)
5. Meanwhile, prepare the black beans and cilantro rice.
6. Remove the meat from the pot and let it cool for about 20 minutes. Remove any visible fat and shred the meat.
7. Drain the pan and place the meat back in it.

8. Prepare the sauce. Place the chilies, enchilada sauce, garlic, and brown sugar in a blender and mix. Add the cola and stir it in with a spoon.
9. Pour the sauce over the meat and jiggle the pan to coat the meat. Place it back in the oven to heat through.
10. To assemble the salad, place a warm flour tortilla on a plate and layer on beans, rice, meat, lettuce, tomato, onion, cheese, guacamole, pico de gallo, sour cream, and cilantro.

Nutrition:

Calories 265

Carbs 2 g

Fat 8.2 g

Protein 11 g

Texas Road House's Mesquite Grilled Pork Chops with Cinnamon Apples

Preparation time: 40 minutes

Cooking time: 40 minutes

Servings: 2

Ingredients:

- Cinnamon Apples
- 4 apples (peeled, sliced)
- 2 tablespoons butter, melted
- 1/3 cup brown sugar
- 2 tablespoons lemon juice
- 3/4 teaspoon cinnamon

- Pork Chops
- 2 pork loin chops with bone, room temperature; 2 inches thick

Paste

- 2 tablespoons extra virgin olive oil
- 2 tablespoons Worcestershire sauce
- 2 teaspoons black pepper, cracked
- 2 teaspoons chili powder
- 2 teaspoons granulated garlic powder
- 2 teaspoons kosher salt
- 1 teaspoon cumin, ground
- 1/2teaspoon cinnamon, ground
- Mesquite wood chips, soaked in water for at least 30 minutes

Directions

1. Prepare the apples by cooking all the cinnamon apple ingredients in butter until the apples soften.
2. When they are ready, set the cooked apples aside. Reheat before serving.
3. Before you begin with the meat, you need to

a) Soak the mesquite chips as instructed;

b) Leave the pork loin at room temperature for 30 to 45 minutes; and

c) Preheat the grill on high.

4. Thoroughly mix all the paste ingredients together. When the paste is done, spread it over the pork chops, covering them completely.
5. Remove the chips from the water and place them in an aluminum foil pan.
6. Place the pan directly over the fire from the grill and cook the pork loin on both sides for about 6 minutes. When the meat is seared, lower the heat to medium.
7. Place the pork over indirect medium heat and cook for another 25 minutes.
8. Remove the pork from heat, wrap it in aluminum foil, and let rest for another 5 minutes.
9. Transfer the pork to a plate with the reheated apples. Serve the entire dish.

Nutrition:

Calories 221

Carbs 2 g

Fat 8.2 g

Protein 12 g

Chi Chi's Pork Tenderloin

Preparation time: 10 minutes

Cooking time: 15 minutes

Servings: 12

Ingredients

- 2 pounds pork tenderloin
- Chi Chi's Bourbon Marinade
- 10 ounces Chi Chi's diced tomatoes with green chilies, drained
- 1/3 cup bourbon
- 1/3 cup soy sauce
- 1/3 cup Worcestershire sauce

- 1 small yellow onion, chopped
- 2 tablespoons honey
- 2 tablespoons mustard
- 1/2teaspoon red pepper flakes

Directions

1. Combine the ingredients for the marinade and place it in a resealable bag.
2. Add the pork and turn to coat. Refrigerate for 8 hours or overnight, turning it from time to time.
3. Preheat the grill or broiler to medium.
4. Remove the meat from the marinade, reserving the marinade.
5. Grill or broil the meat for 7 minutes on each side, or until it reaches 165°F internally.
6. Strain the marinade into a saucepan and bring it to a boil. Simmer for 2–3 minutes and strain. Serve it as a sauce with the meat.

Nutrition:

Calories 251

Carbs 2 g

Fat 8.2 g

Protein 10.3 g

PF Chang's Beef Stew

Preparation Time: 10 minutes

Cooking Time: 2 hours

Servings: 8

Ingredients:

- 1-pound stewing beef, in medium sized chunks
- 3 tablespoons vegetable oil, divided
- Salt and pepper, to taste
- 1/2 cup flour1 onion, chopped
- 4 medium potatoes, cut into chunks
- 5 carrots, peeled and cut into chunks 1-quart beef broth 1/3 cup ketchup
- 1 cup peas

Directions:

1. Mix the flour with salt and pepper to taste and toss with the meat.
2. Add 2 tablespoons of oil to a large pot and over medium high heat brown beef in flour, add all the flour.
3. Stir often so the flour and meat, do not burn, but brown nicely. Remove meat to a plate.
4. Add the last tablespoon of oil and sauté the onion until translucent scraping up a browned bit from the meat.

5. Transfer the meat back to the pot, add the potatoes and carrots. Add the stock and ketchup. Stir well to combine.
6. Simmer over low heat, stirring often for 1 1/2 hours. Adjust seasoning.
7. Add frozen peas just before serving. Stir to defrost and serve.

Nutrition:

Calories: 178,

Carbohydrates: 17g,

Protein: 16g,

Fat: 4g,

Saturated Fat: 2g,

Cholesterol: 35mg,

Sodium: 209mg,

Potassium: 602mg,

Fiber: 3g,

Sugar: 3g

P.F. Chang's Meat Loaf

Preparation Time: 15 minutes

Cooking Time: 1 1/2hours

Servings: 6

Ingredients:

- 2 large eggs
- 2/3 cup whole milk
- 3 slices bread, torn
- 1/2 cup chopped onion
- 1/2 cup grated carrot
- 1 cup shredded cheddar or part-skim mozzarella cheese
- 1 tablespoon minced fresh parsley or
- 1 teaspoon dried parsley
- 1 teaspoon dried basil, thyme, or sage, optional
- 1 teaspoon salt 1/4 teaspoon pepper
- 1-1/2 pounds lean ground beef

TOPPING:

- 1/2 cup tomato sauce 1/2 cup packed brown sugar 1 teaspoon prepared mustard

Directions:

1. In a large bowl, beat eggs. Add milk and bread; let stand until liquid is absorbed. Stir in the onion, carrot, cheese, and seasonings.
2. Crumble beef over mixture and mix well. Shape into a 7-1/2x3-1/2x2-1/2-in. loaf in a shallow baking pan.
3. Bake, uncovered, at 350° for 45 minutes. Combine the topping ingredients, spoon half of the mixture over meat loaf.
4. Bake 30 minutes longer or until meat is no longer pink and a thermometer reads 160°, occasionally spooning remaining topping over loaf. Let stand 10 minutes before serving.

Nutrition:

Calories: 398,

Fat: 17g,

Saturated fat: 9g,

Cholesterol: 164 mg,

P.F. Chang's Roast Beef

Preparation Time: 20 minutes

Cooking Time: 2 1/2hours

Servings: 8

Ingredients:

- 1 tablespoon canola oil
- 1 beef eye round roast (about 2-1/2 pounds)
- 1 garlic clove, minced
- 2 teaspoons dried basil
- 1 teaspoon salt
- 1 teaspoon dried rosemary, crushed
- 1/2 teaspoon pepper
- 1 medium onion, chopped
- 1 teaspoon beef bouillon granules
- 1 cup brewed coffee
- 3/4 cup water
- Gravy:
- 1/4 cup all-purpose flour
- 1/4 cup cold water

Directions:

1. In a Dutch oven, heat oil over medium heat; brown roast on all sides. Remove from pan. Mix garlic and seasonings, sprinkle over roast.
2. Add onion to same pan; cook and stir over medium heat until tender; stir in bouillon, coffee and 3/4 cup water.
3. Add roast; bring to a boil. Reduce heat; simmer, covered, until meat is tender, about 2-1/2 hours. Remove roast from pan, reserving cooking juices. Tent with foil; let stand 10 minutes before slicing.
4. Mix flour and cold water until smooth; stir into cooking juices. Bring to a boil, stirring constantly. Cook and stir until thickened, 1-2 minutes. Serve with roast.

Nutrition:

Calories: 198,

Fat: 6g,

Cholesterol: 65mg,

Sodium: 453mg,

Carbohydrate: 5g,

Protein: 28g

Chapter 8

Dessert Recipes

P.F. Chang's Coconut Pineapple Ice Cream with Banana Spring Rolls

Preparation Time: 5 minutes

Cooking time 30 minutes

Servings 6

Ingredients

Ice cream

- 1 (13½-ounce) jar of coconut milk
- 1 cup of granulated sugar
- 11/2cups of heavy cream
- 1 teaspoon of coconut extract
- 1 (8-ounce) can of crushed pineapple, drained
- 1/3 cup of shredded coconut

Banana spring rolls

- 3 ripe bananas, preferably plantains, halved horizontally
- 3 rice paper or wonton wrappers
- 1–3 tablespoons of brown sugar
- 1 teaspoon of cinnamon
- Oil, for frying
- Caramel sauce, for drizzling (optional)
- Paste for sealing wrappers
- 2 tablespoons of water
- 2 teaspoons of flour or cornstarch

Directions

1. Make the frozen dessert. Place coconut milk and sugar in a bowl. Mix with mixer until sugar is dissolved.
2. Mix in remaining ingredients until well-blended. Place in frozen dessert maker to churn and follow manufacturer's instructions until frozen dessert holds when scooped with a spoon, about a half-hour.
3. Transfer to a container with lid and freeze for a minimum of 2 hours or until desired firmness is reached.

4. Make the banana spring rolls. Lay the wrapper on a flat surface. Position a banana slice near the sting of the wrapper closest to you at rock bottom.
5. Sprinkle with about one teaspoon to 1 tablespoon sugar, depending on how sweet you would like it. Sprinkle with a pinch or two of cinnamon. Roll up sort of a burrito, tucking in the sides. In a small bowl, stir the paste ingredients together.
6. Brush the paste on the sting of the wrapper and seal the roll. Place roll, closed side down, on a plate, and repeat with the remaining bananas. Heat oil, about 1–11/2inches deep, over medium to high heat. Fry the rolls until golden brown, about 1–2 minutes on all sides. Place on paper towels to empty.
7. Serve the rolls with scoops of frozen dessert and drizzle with caramel sauce, if desired.

Nutrition:

Calories: 940

Total Fat: 35g

Carbs: 14g

Protein: 149g

Fiber: 2g

Taco Bell's Pumpkin Cheesecake

Preparation Time: 30 minutes + 8 hours refrigeration time

Cooking Time: 1 hour and 45 minutes

Servings: 8

Ingredients

- 2 1/2cups of graham cracker crumbs
- 3/4 cup of unsalted butter, melted
- 2 3/4 cups of granulated sugar, divided
- 1 teaspoon of salt, plus a pinch
- 4 (8-ounce) blocks of cream cheese, at room temperature
- 1/4cup of sour cream
- 1 (15-ounce) can pure pumpkin
- 6 large eggs, room temperature
- 1 tablespoon of vanilla extract
- 2 1/2teaspoons of ground cinnamon
- 1 teaspoon of ginger, ground
- 1/4teaspoon of cloves, ground
- 2 cups of whipped cream, sweetened
- 1/3 cup of toasted pecans, roughly chopped

Directions

1. Preheat the oven to 325°F and grease a 12-inch springform pan.
2. In a bowl, combine the cracker crumbs, melted butter, 1/4cup of the sugar, and a pinch of salt. Mix until well combined and press the mixture into the prepared springform pan and bake for about 25 minutes.
3. While the crust is baking, begin making the filling by beating together the cheese, soured cream, and pumpkin.
4. Add the remainder of the sugar, and slowly incorporate the beaten eggs and vanilla. Add the remaining salt, cinnamon, ginger, and cloves.
5. Fill an outsized baking pan (big enough to carry your springform pan) with about half an in. of water. Place it in the oven and let the water get hot.
6. Put foil around the edges of your springform pan, then add the filling and place the pan in the oven inside the water bath you made with the baking pan.
7. Bake for 1 hour and 45 minutes, or until the middle is about. You'll turn the foil over the sides of the cake if it starts to urge too brown. Remove the pan from the oven and place it on a cooling rack for a minimum of one hour before removing the edges of the springform pan.

8. After it's cooled, remove the sides and refrigerate the cheesecake for a minimum of 8 hours or overnight.
9. Serve with topping and toasted pecans.

Nutrition:

Calories: 740

Fat: 47g

Carbs: 68g

Fiber: 1g

Sugars: 53g

Protein: 11g

Chipotle's Peach Cobbler

Preparation Time: 10 minutes

Cooking time: 45 minutes

Servings: 4

Ingredients:

- 11/4cups Bisquick
- 1 cup milk
- 1/2cup melted butter
- 1/4teaspoon nutmeg
- 1/2teaspoon cinnamon
- Vanilla ice cream, for serving

Filling:

- 1 (30-ounce) can peaches in syrup, drained
- 1/4cup sugar

Topping:

- 1/2cup brown sugar
- 1/4cup almond slices
- 1/2teaspoon cinnamon
- 1 tablespoon melted butter

Directions:

1. Preheat the oven to 375°F.
2. Grease the bottom and sides of an 8×8-inch pan.
3. Whisk together the Bisquick, milk, butter, nutmeg and cinnamon in a large mixing bowl. When thoroughly combined, pour into the greased baking pan.
4. Mix together the peaches and sugar in another mixing bowl. Put the filling on top of the batter in the pan. Bake for about 45 minutes.
5. In another bowl, mix together the brown sugar, almonds, cinnamon, and melted butter. After the cobbler has cooked for 45 minutes, cover evenly with the topping and bake for an additional 10 minutes.
6. Serve with a scoop of vanilla ice cream.

Nutrition:

Calories: 446

Fat: 12.6 g

Carbs: 21. 2 g

Protein: 21.1 g

Sodium: 300 mg

Royal Dansk Butter Cookies

Preparation Time: 15 minutes

Cooking Time: 25 minutes

Servings: 10

Ingredients:

- 120g cake flour, sifted
- 1/2teaspoon vanilla extract
- 25g powdered sugar
- 120g softened butter, at room temperature
- A pinch of sea salt, approximately 1/4teaspoon

Directions:

1. Using a hand mixer; beat the butter with sugar, vanilla & salt until almost doubled in mass & lightened to a yellowish-white in color, for 8 to 10 minutes, on low to middle speed.
2. Scrape the mixture from the sides of yours bowl using a rubber spatula. Sift the flour x 3 times & gently fold in until well incorporated.
3. Transfer the mixture into a sheet of plastic wrap, roll into log & cut a hole on it; placing it into the piping bag attached with a nozzle flower tips 4.6cm/1.81" x 1.18".

4. Pipe each cookie into 5cm wide swirls on a parchment paper lined baking tray.
5. Cover & place them in a freezer until firm up, for 30 minutes.
6. Preheat your oven to 300 F in advance. Once done; bake until the edges start to turn golden, for 20 minutes.
7. Let completely cool on the cooling rack before serving.
8. Store them in an airtight container.

Nutrition:

Calories: 220

Fat: 8.8 g

Carbs: 22. 3 g

Protein: 30.2 g

Sodium: 200 mg

Campfire S'mores

Preparation Time: 15 minutes

Cooking time: 40 minutes

Servings: 9

Ingredients:

- Graham Cracker Crust
- 2 cups graham cracker crumbs
- 1/4cup sugar
- 1/2cup butter
- 1/2teaspoon cinnamon
- 1 small package brownie mix (enough for an 8×8-inch pan), or use the brownie ingredients listed below.

Brownie Mix:

- 1/2cup flour
- 1/3 cup cocoa
- 1/4teaspoon baking powder
- 1/4teaspoon salt
- 1/2cup butter
- 1 cup sugar
- 1 teaspoon vanilla
- 2 large eggs

S'mores Topping:

- 9 large marshmallows
- 5 Hershey candy bars
- 41/2cups vanilla ice cream
- 1/2cup chocolate sauce

Directions:

1. Preheat the oven to 350°F.
2. Mix together the graham cracker crumbs, sugar, cinnamon and melted butter in a medium bowl. Stir until the crumbs and sugar have combined with the butter.
3. Line an 8×8-inch baking dish with parchment paper. Make sure to use enough so that you'll be able to lift the baked brownies out of the dish easily. Press the graham cracker mixture into the bottom of the lined pan.
4. Place pan in the oven to prebake the crust a bit while you are making the brownie mixture.
5. Melt the butter over medium heat in a large saucepan, then stir in the sugar and vanilla. Whisk in the eggs one at a time. Then whisk in the dry ingredients, followed by the nuts. Mix until smooth. Take the crust out of the oven, pour the mixture into it, and bake for 23–25 minutes. When brownies are done, remove from oven and let cool in the pan.

6. After the brownies have cooled completely, lift them out of the pan using the edges of the parchment paper. Be careful not to crack or break the brownies. Cut into individual slices.
7. When you are ready to serve, place a marshmallow on top of each brownie and broil in the oven until the marshmallow starts to brown. You can also microwave for a couple of seconds, but you won't get the browning that you would in the broiler.
8. Remove from the oven and top each brownie with half of a Hershey bar. Serve with ice cream and a drizzle of chocolate sauce.

Nutrition:

Calories: 623

Fat: 14.8 g

Carbs: 10. 2 g

Protein: 39.0 g

Sodium: 231 mg

Chipotle's Banana Pudding

Preparation Time: 15 minutes

Cooking time 5 minutes

Servings: 10

Ingredients:

- 6 cups milk
- 5 eggs, beaten
- 1/4teaspoon vanilla extract
- 11/8cups flour
- 11/2cups sugar
- 3/4 pound vanilla wafers
- 3 bananas, peeled
- 8 ounces Cool Whip or 2 cups of whipped cream

Directions:

1. In a large saucepan, heat the milk to about 170°F.
2. Mix the eggs, vanilla, flour, and sugar together in a large bowl.
3. Very slowly add the egg mixture to the warned milk and cook until the mixture thickens to a custard consistency.

4. Layer the vanilla wafers to cover the bottom of a baking pan or glass baking dish. You can also use individual portion dessert dish or glasses.
5. Layer banana slices over the top of the vanilla wafers. Be as liberal with the bananas as you want.
6. Layer the custard mixture on top of the wafers and bananas. Move the pan to the refrigerator and cool for 11/2hours. When ready to serve, spread Cool Whip (or real whipped cream, if you prefer) over the top. Garnish with banana slices and wafers if desired.

Nutrition:

Calories: 312

Fat: 2.8 g

Carbs: 4.2 g

Protein: 6.0 g

Sodium: 329 mg

Conclusion

Now that you're ready to recreate your favorite foods at home, you may want to make this a regular part of your culinary adventure. Here are some important tips and ideas to keep in mind as you go through this volume:

Take your time and don't rush. Some recipes are quick and can be made in minutes, though it's best to slow down and not rush beforehand. After more than once or twice, you'll know exactly how long it takes to prepare your favorite dishes.

When making your shopping list, include all the basic items first, followed by any additives or special items for specific recipes or meals. This can be an easy way to keep your budget and avoid overspending, especially when it's tempting. Many of the restaurant recipes are made with common ingredients and don't need to come from items not found in most stores or markets.

Invite your family and friends to participate in the recreation of your favorite restaurants. They may have some great ideas and suggestions for preparing new foods and variations to try.

Don't expect every recipe to be perfect the first time! Sometimes the type of oven or a small change in ingredients can make a significant difference. This can be an easy way to keep your budget and avoid overspending, especially when it's tempting.

Many of the restaurant recipes are made with common ingredients and don't need to come from items not found in most stores or markets.

For this reason, buying common meals, as well as these recipes, should be simple and easy to manage.

When grocery shopping, bring a list with you and a friend, neighbor or family member so you can both work together to choose ingredients. Preparing and buying food with others is a good tradition in some communities, which can be extended to this opportunity.

Never give up, as some recipes can be a bit difficult or challenging at first until you get used to the method.

If you're not sure about a particular recipe for that reason, something you've never tried before (either the recipe or the food), make a small portion and buy enough for one batch or meal. That way, you can test it out yourself to see if it's worth making again. Also, make enough samples with friends and family to see how much they like it.

CPSIA information can be obtained
at www.ICGtesting.com
Printed in the USA
BVHW021012150321
602551BV00009B/646

9 781802 23853